While in recent years the role and experience of animals during the First World War has become better known, the story of how animals in Britain were involved in and affected by the global conflict that broke out a generation later is relatively unfamiliar.

Animals played a significant part in late 1930s Britain, and the approach and outbreak of war prompted responses by those charities, professionals and institutions involved with them. One particular reaction was called 'the September Holocaust of 1939' by contemporaries – the reluctant but deliberate mass destruction of much-loved pets by their owners. This was so their animals might avoid the suffering inflicted by the expected (albeit not forthcoming) prolonged air attacks on cities once war had been declared.

The war on the Home Front affected zoos, farms, country estates and pets, which animal-related charities strove to rescue. Animals also became important as a food source for the survival of rationed Britain.

Women at Melton Mowbray train horses to wear a harness and pack in preparation for war.

Horses, mules, camels, dogs and birds participated in the war itself, and some performed so outstandingly that they were considered 'heroes', prompting the creation of an animal VC. In the spirit of remembrance, it is right to look at their roles and consider what they achieved.

ANIMALS IN BRITAIN IN 1939

Britain in the 1930s was renowned for its love of animals. As today, many people encountered them in their daily lives, either as pets or by visiting zoos and circuses. And animals also featured in hobbies and leisure activities – pigeon fancying, and horse and greyhound racing were popular at this time. Animals still played a part in employment too, notably on the farm and down the coal mine. Other animals – famously the Dartmoor and Shetland ponies – remained in the wild. All such creatures, wherever they might be found, would be affected by the outbreak of war in September 1939.

The horse was still a familiar presence in 1930s urban centres and, although less so, industrial sites. Thus while horse-drawn buses and trams were no longer used in London (besides a few hansom cabs – the last licence not relinquished until 1947) horses were still to be found on the streets of the capital and other major centres. Their chief role was as 'vanners' – pulling carts or wagons for collecting or delivering, primarily to people's homes. There were, for instance, thousands of horse-drawn milk floats, as well as coal and rag-and-bone carts. Similarly, not just the London termini but almost every railway station in Britain still had at least two or three horses. The railway companies were still major users of horses, employing more of them (11,163) in 1938 than motor vehicles (10,367). They were used mainly for shunting, as well as carrying passengers and luggage.

Mick the Miller, a champion racing greyhound in the years leading up to war.

In 1939 there were more cart horses than tractors on British farms and fox hunting continued to be popular. In 1929 The Pony Club was established to encourage children to ride horses. Ten years later it had over 10,000 members.

Several major animal charities were active in the 1930s, concerned primarily but not exclusively with animal welfare in Britain. Campaigns overseas included the cruel conditions experienced by tortoises transported from North Africa, and the successful purchase of 118 First World War horses and 483 mules from Belgium. There were on-going campaigns too against blood sports and the use of animals in scientific research.

Horse shows were popular before the war.

There were relatively few animals in the armed forces in 1939. Some 16 cavalry regiments in the UK still used horses in addition to tanks; the equines numbered approximately 4,000 and were cared for by the Royal Army Veterinary Corps (RAVC). Both the RAVC and the number of horses would increase during the Second World War.

The city of London still provided horse troughs in the street in 1939.

THE APPROACH OF WAR

Fears of chemical attack led to gas masks and respirators being designed for dogs and horses.

Many believed that the Great War (1914–18) would prove to be 'the war to end war', but by the mid-1930s the prospect of another conflict was growing. In March 1936 the Royal Society for the Prevention of Cruelty to Animals (RSPCA) began planning for animal casualties in the event of war. It was widely believed that the next conflict would involve immediate heavy bombing and gas attacks. In 1937 the Society published *Air Raid Precautions for Animals*; 100,000 copies were issued. It included details of equipment to help save animals – from livestock and working animals to pets – trapped and frightened because of fire or bombed buildings. Featured in the booklet was the 'dog and cat grasper', which comprised a running noose attached to a long handle to enable the rescue of frightened or inaccessible animals with a quick-release device to free the trapped animal.

The Munich Crisis in September 1938 led many people to fear that war was imminent and prompted some to evacuate their pets to the countryside. During the Crisis some 700 people visited and 3,000 telephoned the RSPCA.

Such was the fear for their safety that there was a demand for gas masks for pets. Although discouraged by the RSPCA, who instead recommended feeding pets a sedative tablet and swathing them in a blanket, such masks were purchased nevertheless, including an expensive (£9) version from Germany. One enquirer was, however, successfully dissuaded from buying masks for their bees. The People's Dispensary for Sick Animals (PDSA) developed a gas-proof kennel with bellows for the pet to operate, at a cost of £4.

Picasso's mural depicting Guernica.

Fear over the effect of heavy bombing was understandable given the attack on Guernica during the Spanish Civil War in April 1937. Picasso's work of that name illustrated the suffering of a horse and a bull, which added to an increased awareness of how animals would suffer in war. The RSPCA was also anxious over the plight of animals in Czechoslovakia following Germany's complete annexation of the country by March 1939. The Society liaised with its German counterpart over animal welfare matters in the event of sustained bombing.

In the aftermath of Kristallnacht, the nationwide attacks on Jews and their property in Germany in November 1938, many Jews sought refuge in the UK, bringing their pets with them. Both the Cats Protection League and Our Dumb Friends League (ODFL – later renamed the Blue Cross) often paid any quarantine fees for animals. There was widespread fear that if left behind in Nazi Germany these animals would be used for scientific experiments.

THE SEPTEMBER MASSACRES

This couple take their bull terrier on a country walk in 1939.

Pet owners were already anxious about the imminence and nature of war in 1938 and because of the anticipated intense bombing and gas attacks some owners decided it would be better to have their pets destroyed.

It was not just the likelihood of war that led pet owners to act in this way. The number of these humane killings was also increased by rumours and misunderstandings of government policy. In August the government had established the National Air Raid Precautions Animals Committee (NARPAC). Soon after, it issued *Advice to Animal Owners*, a pamphlet that urged pet owners, in the event of war, to evacuate their animals. Failing that, the pamphlet claimed, 'it really is kindest to have them destroyed'. It recommended the CASH Captive bolt pistol as one way to achieve this. According to the accompanying advertisement, the pistol provided, 'the speediest, most efficient and reliable means of destroying any animal … cats and all sizes of dogs'. This advice also featured in most newspapers and on the radio. The RSPCA, PDSA, the Battersea Dogs and Cats Home and other animal charities and organisations opposed such killing.

Nevertheless, given the apparent government advice and fears over what war might bring, together with the prospect of animal food shortages, many decided to end their pets'

Horses
In dispatching horses, errors are mainly due to the operator aiming too low. Place the muzzle of the pistol against the forehead skin immediately below the roots of the forelock. (See Fig. 1.)

FIG. 1.

Cattle
Cattle of all classes should be neck-roped or haltered. Draw imaginary lines from the base of each horn to the eye on the opposite side and aim at the spot where these lines cross. (See Fig. 2.)

Sheep
Aim at the centre line of the forehead between the levels of the ears and eyes. Another position is midway between the ears, aiming straight down towards the gullet. (See Fig. 3.)

Horned Sheep
Place the muzzle in the centre line immediately behind

A pamphlet outlines how best to dispatch different animals in a humane way.

The National Air Raid Precautions Animals Committee introduced these animal identity discs.

lives or abandon them to the care of others. As a result, vets, animal charities and the Battersea home were inundated with owners' requests for their pets to be adopted or destroyed.

Nationally, nearly one million animals were destroyed in the first week of September 1939. In one night alone some 200,000 dogs were put to death. Animal carcasses lay in heaps outside veterinary surgeries. The RSPCA's history revealed that destructors could not burn the bodies fast enough because furnaces were not allowed to operate during the blackout. Some 80,000 animals were disposed of in secret mass burial grounds in London's East End alone. Some animals were more fortunate. One abandoned dog – a chow called Baerchen, left behind by German embassy staff – was offered a home by over 200 people. Some vets, rather than put down healthy animals, moved to where evacuees and their pets had been relocated.

PETS WHO SURVIVED: PROSPECTS BEFORE THE BLITZ

In the aftermath of what the National Canine Defence League (later renamed Dogs Trust) called at the time 'the September Holocaust', 'In Memoriam' notices appeared for animals that had been destroyed. Contemporaneously, *The Times* (7 September) reported that it was compulsory for pets to be destroyed but voiced concern that the destruction of cats would result in a huge increase in vermin (as experienced in Madrid during the Spanish Civil War of 1936–39). Such comment, while adding to the distress of those who had lost their pets, might reassure those whose animals still lived. But owners remained anxious.

The government had made it clear before the war that, unlike with children, it would not assist in the evacuation of pets.

Mrs Day's cat Little One is wearing a NARPAC collar, which was meant to ensure that, if he got lost during a blackout, he could be returned to his owner.

They were their owners' responsibility. Also, pets housed on school premises should be evacuated with the pupils or destroyed unless the caretaker took them on. However, the RSPCA often came to the rescue. It now took charge of not only rabbits, cats and dogs, but birds, guinea pigs and even alligators.

The ODFL established a fostering scheme whereby people adopted animals from major cities or those unable to accompany evacuees for the duration of the war. Newspapers and animal publications carried advertisements both appealing for and offering accommodation. Weekly charges levied by the Animal Defence Society ranged from 10 shillings (50p today) for a dog to 1d (less than 0.5p) for a budgerigar. Advice was

A dog wears a striped black and white coat to ensure visibility during blackouts in the early weeks of the Second World War.

When the Blitz did start, some were lucky to survive.

also sought – for example, how to protect fish in open-air garden pools. The owner of six goldfish asked a cinema proprietor in North London to add their fish to the ornamental pool in the foyer for the duration of the war.

The blackout started the night war broke out. This meant that no lighting should be visible from outside a property, and the streets were vigorously policed to enforce this. Among those who came before the courts was an engineer who claimed that his cat had turned on the light attached to his electric tea maker. Another was fined for showing the light of his goldfish bowl. The roads were completely dark too. Dogs were not allowed to wander the streets during the blackout because they were a possible danger to pedestrians, cyclists and motorists. Still, many mishaps occurred, including pedestrians tripping over (invisible) leads of dogs being taken for their evening walks.

9

UNDER ATTACK:
PETS AND URBAN AIR RAIDS

The long-awaited and much-feared air raids began in earnest in September 1940. Pet owners' preparation had, in some cases, included some training for their animals – familiarising them with garden shelters, for instance. Nevertheless it was still a difficult time for both pet owner and pet.

Pet owners often believed, perhaps rightly, that not only did their cats and dogs become used to the raids but they soon learned to recognise the sound of the air-raid siren – even to distinguish between the 'warning' and the 'all clear' signals. Also, because of their acute hearing, some dogs could detect approaching aircraft before their owners and alerted them accordingly. Some people even credited their survival during particular attacks to their pets' responses.

Less appreciated were those pets that helped themselves to any available food abandoned in their owners' rush to take

The first mass German air raid on London, September 1940.

cover. As expected, cats were particularly skilled in finishing off fish suppers. Budgerigars would become overexcited by both the noise and increased family activity during a raid. Many had been taught to squawk 'Damn Hitler!' in these circumstances.

It was illegal to take animals (other than guide dogs) into public shelters or underground stations when they were being used as cover from air attacks, although some pet owners entering public shelters would hide their animals in baskets or clothing. Some householders displayed cards offering their willingness to give sanctuary in their own shelters to dog walkers caught outside in daylight raids. People were urged to offer empty garages as temporary refuge for any passing horses. The Royal Mews, neighbouring Buckingham Palace, offered stabling during air raids.

Londoners exercising their dogs in Kensington Gardens could take their pets to a special air-raid shelter, where the dogs were protected in small cubicles.

Homes often displayed details of those who lived there, together with any pets and the rooms where everyone slept. This information made it easier for search parties and animal-rescue squads to look for and identify casualties in damaged properties. Some people who subsequently decided to abandon their bombed-out homes might leave their pets tied to outside posts for passers-by to adopt. Other pets might be freed, harmed or killed by an air raid. Even a nearby attack, as opposed to a direct hit, might shatter goldfish bowls or fish tanks, killing their occupants as a consequence.

IMPORTANT!

NO. OF PERSONS SLEEPING IN THIS HOUSE

DOG / CAT
(Cross out whichever is inapplicable)

ALSO **IN**

HOUSE
HIS BED IS

(State location of bed as exactly as possible.)

Issued by
The National Canine   The Royal Society for the
Defence League,   Prevention of Cruelty
Victoria Station House,   to Animals,
S.W.1.   105, Jermyn Street, S.W.1.

This leaflet could be fixed to the gatepost of a house to alert rescuers of the presence of domestic pets.

TO THE RESCUE

When the lights failed at the ODFL depot, first aid was still given to this dog who had suffered in the Blitz.

Britain under attack had a major impact on the work of animal organisations. The demands on staff and volunteers ranged from giving advice about how to calm animals during raids (by feeding them a sedative) to rescuing those that had been trapped or injured – and doing so amid the danger of collapsed buildings and unexploded bombs.

By 1939, the RSPCA and PDSA had between them a national network of over 100 centres. Originally, the purpose of these organisations was to care for sick and homeless animals. This continued but the conflict also brought additional care responsibilities. Consequently PDSA established first-aid posts. They were staffed from the moment an alert sounded and would care for animals during and after a raid – the treatment administered by candlelight during the blackout. Typically, the ODFL hospital in London Victoria not only cared for sick animals, but also acted as a temporary animal refuge for pet owners on their way to public air-raid shelters. During 1939–45 it admitted over 45,000 animals to be treated, boarded or destroyed.

During and after an air attack animal-rescue squads would search for pets and other creatures trapped among the new debris. If injured they would be taken away by animal ambulances, which were available in London and other major centres. This work could be dangerous: a dog and canary were rescued from a house where one hour later a delayed-action bomb exploded. Often, rescue was made more difficult by the understandably uncooperative behaviour of the animals themselves. But joyful reunions of frightened pets with tearful, anxious owners would have compensated for this. During the course of the war the RSPCA rescued almost 200 horses, 600 sheep and hundreds of pigs, cats and dogs nationally.

The societies comforted animal owners during raids both by offering their animals temporary care and by reassuring those resigned to their own imminent death but anxious over the long-term future of the pets they would leave behind. The ODFL centre in Hammersmith, London, alone dealt with the latter situation over a dozen times during the war.

Animal organisations were themselves not immune from attack. Some 11 RSPCA clinics, and ODFL centres in North and East London, Eastbourne and Portsmouth suffered wartime damage. Some of the League's dogs escaped from their kennels at Blackheath, London, when a blast demolished the centre's walls and fences. All animals were later caught.

Iris Davis, a volunteer worker for the ODFL, rescued around 600 stray cats during the war using her 'lassoo'.

A cat is rescued from a bombed house and sent back to a NARPAC post in a hand cart, November 1940.

13

ON THE FARM AND IN THE BACKYARD

Pets and working animals were not the only creatures to be affected by the war. By the 1930s Britain relied on imports to feed her population adequately, but the war reduced these supplies significantly. Rationing was introduced in January 1940 but this didn't solve the problem. Britain needed to increase its own food production, particularly its supply of meat and poultry. Government policy and the public's response in both town and country made this possible.

Both arable and pastoral farming continued during the war but both underwent major changes. In 1939 there were 650,000 horses on British farms, used mainly for ploughing, and about 50,000 tractors. Primarily due to government wartime policy to maximise the use of land and agricultural labour, the number of tractors was increased by 400 per cent while the number of horses halved. Similarly, fewer pigs were reared on farms as dairy cattle were preferred.

A Land Girl examines the health of the chicken she is holding on a poultry farm.

Campaigns urged people to 'Dig for Victory' and many began to grow or increase their cultivation of fruit and vegetables. Although relatively few people, especially in urban areas where around 80 per cent of the population lived, had much experience of raising poultry and livestock, many now undertook the challenge. The government immediately instructed local authorities to override restrictions on keeping these food sources in

Whatever your FRONT LINE JOB

This is your
SECOND LINE JOB

LEND A HAND
ON THE LAND

parks and domestic gardens. The Ministry of Food recommended people rear animals such as hens, ducks, geese, rabbits, goats, pigs and bees. Government leaflets, radio programmes and specialist bodies provided advice on the care of these animals.

By 1945 the Domestic Poultry Keepers' Council had 1.25 million members (responsible for 12 million birds) and accounted for around 25 per cent of the nation's official fresh egg supplies. People also formed their own animal clubs: there were 6,900 pig clubs in the UK. In London, the Royal Park staff raised pigs in Hyde Park and National Fire Service members established a rabbitry in Mayfair.

Sugar was rationed in January 1940, but this did not affect beekeepers who were permitted to buy sugar to feed bees in winter. One apiary near a jam factory produced pink honey because the bees had been licking the jam. Beekeepers were anxious about air raids, not least because bomb fumes caused the bees to swarm, so during air raids chloroform rags might be used to stupefy and thus confine them. After a raid at Plymouth, Brother Adam, a renowned German-born beekeeper at Buckfast Abbey, was (falsely) suspected of communicating with the Luftwaffe with his arrangement of hives on Dartmoor.

Cattle were a popular animal to farm during the war.

STAYING ALIVE: ANIMAL FOOD

Even kitchen waste could help the war effort when put to practical use.

Backyard pigs, poultry and rabbits might supplement the dining-room table, but families often found it difficult to eat those animals they had nurtured. Nevertheless, each rabbit provided about 2.5lb of meat when four months old and their skins could be sewn into children's coats or slippers; goose and hen feathers were used to repair eiderdowns. More critically, as the war situation became desperate and food was short there was increasing debate over whether pet ownership, especially of cats and dogs, should be allowed to continue.

The prospect of allocating scarce food resources to pets in time of war was controversial even before the conflict began. Some of those who had destroyed their pets had done so because they feared the animals might otherwise starve. The production of pet food was reduced and soon became difficult to obtain. Furthermore, very little of the meat ration could be fed to dogs and it was illegal to give them butchers' meat bones. Instead such bones were assigned to street swill or pig bins, which, despite being covered, soon attracted dogs who learnt how to overturn and raid them.

The RSPCA provided recipes for dog food that did not include anything rationed. These recipes often used horsemeat, which was sprayed green to deter sale for human consumption. Nevertheless, overall consumption of horsemeat increased, partly because it was being falsely labelled as beef. The meat of cattle injured or killed in air raids was also condemned and dyed, although people living nearby often secured a portion before this happened.

Feeding the animals in Melton Mowbray in 1943.

Guide dogs were more fortunate. As a result of battle injury or bombing, more people lost their sight than in peacetime and consequently the number of guide dogs increased. In 1940–41 some 45 people were blinded as a result of air raids, but there was no increase in the number of dogs trained annually (23). The government, however, permitted a special ration for dogs undergoing training – existing owners had a special monthly allowance of 35lb of cereal dog food.

It was illegal to give milk to cats (although policing this was difficult); water had to suffice. After being lobbied, Parliament permitted damaged dried milk to be given to those cats reducing vermin in warehouses and elsewhere. One cat, it was claimed, on learning that it was to be destroyed, caught a wild rabbit, and continued to do so subsequently.

Cats had their uses, but canaries (along with budgerigars and parrots), it was argued, did not. Some maintained that such birds boosted morale. Information was provided on how to grow seeds for canaries and how to raise mealworms (which had previously been imported from Germany). It was illegal to give bread to wild birds, although people often did so – surreptitiously.

Rabbits were a good food source.

ZOOS IN WARTIME

Zoos were alert to the prospect of war for at least several months before it broke out and prepared accordingly. This involved deciding which animals would be kept and how they would dispose of the remainder. Whipsnade Zoo, for instance, had agreed to take London Zoo's lions and tigers in the event of war and had already acquired the necessary wire netting to enclose them.

On 3 September 1939, the government required all places of entertainment, including zoos, to close indefinitely because of the immediate and intensive bombing that was expected. As such bombing did not happen, places reopened – Whipsnade on 9 September and London Zoo soon afterwards. But action had been taken and precautions remained in place. Edinburgh Zoo's poisonous snakes had been killed and London Zoo soon chloroformed its poisonous snakes and invertebrates. Its aquarium was drained of 200,000 gallons of water because of the risk of broken glass and flooding if the zoo was hit. Some fish were transferred but most were bottled for museums or eaten. Vacated sites had new uses: rabbits, for instance – bred for their meat and fur – occupied the snake dens.

London Zoo chloroformed its poisonous snakes.

Some zoos were patrolled by riflemen during air raids to shoot any animals that might escape in the event of the zoo being hit. Between September and December 1940 both London Zoo and Whipsnade were hit. Some birds escaped from London Zoo and a giraffe and antelope died. The reptile house was hit during the 'Little Blitz' in summer 1944. In the event of an air raid, visitors were allowed to shelter in the zoo's basements.

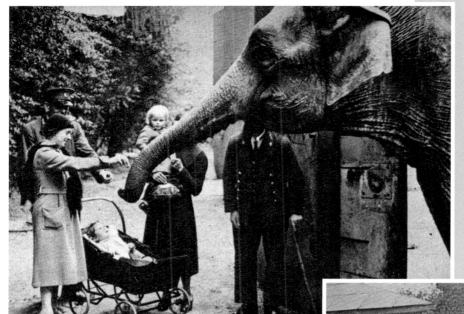

But London Zoo's visitor numbers fell – due in part to some mothers and children being evacuated from the capital; also, unnecessary travel was discouraged. Similarly, there were fewer zoo staff as many were employed in the armed forces. Some zoos held war-related exhibitions – for example, on vermin destruction, and keeping poultry and pigs. Some zoo staff organised their own pig clubs.

Bristol Zoo, as well as London and Belfast Zoos, was particularly vulnerable to air attack. Most of its big cats were transferred to Chester Zoo and its polar bears were killed – their enclosure became an air-raid shelter. To help with feeding costs, Bristol, like London Zoo, encouraged the public to sponsor or adopt animals. Food supplies for animals were problematic, especially fish. Penguins and seals were persuaded to eat meat soaked in cod-liver oil. Meanwhile, visitors might steal waterfowl eggs. One visitor to Bristol Zoo noticed a monkey rebuilding a banana skin and looking longingly at it, although it only contained a small potato.

This air-raid shelter went under the Rodent House at London Zoo.

ANIMAL-BASED LEISURE PURSUITS

Controversy surrounded greyhound racing during the war.

Hunting, coursing and shooting continued throughout the war but in many areas it was reduced or even temporarily abandoned. War agricultural committees determined the rations allocated to each hunting pack of hounds (known as a 'kennel') and this was reduced further as the war progressed; some kennels were destroyed as a result of the meagre rations.

Hostility towards hunting continued and its difficulties grew – not least over the issue of feeding the dogs and securing supplies amid the shortage. The League Against Cruel Sports saw hunting as unpatriotic. Furthermore, temporary airfields and army camps also meant there was less land available for hunting. Even the increase in ploughed land added to the difficulties of hunting, as under these circumstances a fox's scent is more easily lost.

Nevertheless, some packs struggled on. Masters and lady masters of the fox hounds took on their full costs and often had to scrounge meat for them; farmers might oblige with carcasses that were deemed unfit for human consumption. Sometimes a pack might be retained for breeding purposes but its size would be cut significantly through destruction or dispersal of surplus hounds. Consequently, it was increasingly difficult for traditional hunting to control the fox population and farmers established their own fox destruction societies. One such society in the Pennines paid £1 for every dead fox presented.

During the war stag hunting with hounds was popular. This took place in Somerset and Devon, and enjoyed government support – venison was an important source of protein. Deer might also destroy root crops such as swedes and turnips. Traditionally deer had been lassoed and their throats cut at the end of the hunt. During the war it was usual for them to be shot.

Horse racing continued during the war but on a reduced scale, with some racecourses no longer available due to requisitioning. This included Aintree and Epsom racecourses. The government wanted the 1940 Derby to be cancelled but it was eventually held at Newmarket – its location for the remainder of the war. However, National Hunt racing was forbidden from September 1942 and steeple chasing was abandoned until January 1945.

Controversy raged both in terms of the resources devoted to horse racing and the widely believed misuse of limited petrol and public transport by spectators. In 1939 there were 2,000 racehorses, each said to consume 10–15lb of grain daily – the total amount equalling an army division's daily ration. There were similar concerns over greyhound racing. As well as meat, it was claimed that such dogs were fed 100 tonnes of grain annually (as wholemeal bread) at a time when professional poultry keepers went short.

Crowds watch a wartime Derby run at Newmarket, June 1941.

British servicemen watch jockey Sam Wragg ride Pont l'Eveque to victory in the 1940 Derby held at Newmarket.

IN THE LINE OF FIRE: HORSES, MULES AND CAMELS

By 1939 all regular mounted regiments operating in Britain, with the exception of the Household Cavalry, had replaced their horses with armoured vehicles. Nevertheless, horses and other animals played a part on the war front. The Royal Army Veterinary Corps (RAVC), having diminished over the years since 1920, underwent a five-fold expansion during the Second World War.

The German army had 35,000 horses when Hitler came to power in 1933 and perhaps half a million horses in 1939, some of which had been imported from Britain and Ireland. The number of horses in the British army only increased in 1939 (from 2,600 to 11,600). Some RAVC staff were assigned to the Chemical Defence Experimental Station at Porton Down in Wiltshire. Their task was to investigate how biological air attacks might affect horses and mules, and to develop anti-gas protection for them.

Servicemen administer medicine to a horse by using a stomach tube.

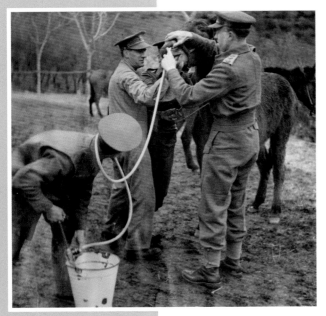

Horses, mules and camels were active in various war zones. Similarly RAVC and RSPCA staff were on active service. The Cypriot Pack Transport (Mule) Company and Indian Mule Transport Companies provided the British Expeditionary Force fighting in France and Flanders with some 3,000 mules in January 1940. This was primarily to assist motor vehicles carrying ammunition and stores. However, the mules' lack of shoes in the icy conditions caused many problems.

As it was not possible to evacuate the animals from Dunkirk in 1940, animal welfare staff cut halter ropes to allow them to fend for themselves until captured by the enemy. Soon after D-Day (June 1944), horse transport – mainly animals captured by the Allies – was used to ease the strain on motor vehicles. The RAVC rounded up thousands of horses abandoned by Germany following their defeat at the Battle of the Falaise Pocket in August 1944. During 1939–45 the Corps cared for 40,000 animals in France.

Mules were important in other parts of Europe and elsewhere. The Greek army deployed some 20,000 mules in 1941; the British and Americans also used many thousands in Tunisia and Italy. In Burma 500 horses and 3,000 mules were transported to the jungle by air. Sometimes mules were drugged and dropped by parachute. As braying could alert the enemy, horses and mules often had their vocal chords cut. It was in Burma, in March 1942, that the final cavalry charge of the British Empire took place. Most of the 60-strong patrol under Captain Sandeman was killed by Japanese infantry.

Donkeys were used to deliver letters and parcels to servicemen in Italy, 1944.

India imported 35,500 mules, ponies and donkeys from South Africa. It provided some 3,600 camels to support other Empire territories; they were used by the Indian army and in British Somaliland to help re-establish the Somaliland Camel Corps following the colony's temporary defeat by Italy in 1940–41.

The Northern Command's Pack Transport Company's job was to transport supplies and ammunition to the infantry over country where wheeled transport was impossible.

DOGS AND THE WAR EFFORT

Although dogs had played a useful role in the First World War, notably on the Western Front, their use by the British military ended with the signing of the Anglo-Irish Treaty in December 1921. Improved telecommunications led military command to conclude that messenger dogs were obsolete. No British schools of instruction for military dogs operated during the interwar era, but they were to be re-established soon after the Second World War broke out.

The War Dog Training School was initially located at the major army barracks in Aldershot, Surrey, but was later moved to the Greyhound Racing Association's centre at Northaw, Hertfordshire. This had excellent medical facilities and was able to cure canine throat infections, which developed as a consequence of the dogs barking constantly on arrival at the school. The Ministry of Aircraft Production's need for dogs to protect its sites was so great that it established its own training school in Cheltenham, Gloucestershire.

Female dog handlers in Northaw, Hertfordshire.

The army estimated that it needed 2,000 dogs, and the Admiralty only 200. Dogs were sourced mainly from animal refuge centres and approximately 6,000 were offered by private owners. America sent over Husky dogs. About half of all dogs offered were successfully trained. Dogs needed to be in good health and unafraid of gunfire. The Alsatian was the preferred breed and became the established dog of the military and security forces. It was seen as strong, intelligent and easy to train – notably for guard duties. Alsatians also performed well as messengers (travelling up to five miles), and carrying out tracker and patrol functions. They were less effective in detecting war casualties or mines. Due to their various skills, dogs accompanied the D-Day landings.

A handler of the British Army of the Rhine with his dog.

It was said that a well-trained guard dog and its handler could free up to eight men from sentry duties. Therefore such dogs were used at home and on active service. Duties on the Home Front included guarding prisoner-of-war camps and protecting an all-female searchlight team in North London. Dogs also assisted sentries in their guarding of ammunition dumps. Animals assigned to protect Vulnerable Points were known as VP dogs. Overseas, infantry patrols might escape ambush because their accompanying dogs had alerted them to the enemy's presence.

Second World War mechanical mine detectors only worked if the mines contained a metal element. Germany soon developed mines that only used glass, wood or plastic. However, Labradors could smell explosives and so could detect mines irrespective of the material used or their location.

This dog is prepared for the task of detecting mines.

BIRDS AND THE WAR

A wireless operator of an Avro Lancaster bomber carries two pigeon boxes. Homing pigeons served as a means of communication in the event of a crash, ditching or radio failure.

Birds were both victims and heroes of the conflict. On the Home Front thousands may have been killed during air raids, and the blast and fires that ensued. But one species of bird, the humble pigeon, was to be a lifesaver.

On the Home Front food shortages were a problem for birds as well as people. It was illegal to feed bread to wild birds but the RSPCA provided details of suitable weeds and other permitted seeds. Converting grassland to arable meant fewer insects for rooks who now consumed winter wheat instead. Consequently the government ordered their destruction – it was suggested that the Home Guard might use their nests as target practice. Birds were also shot for food. One London meat market was known to sell rooks, sparrows and seagulls, as well as the more familiar grouse, pheasant and partridge.

Air raids initially terrified birds but, gradually, they became accustomed to them. Starlings continued to roost in London during the Blitz, although woodpigeons, often shot because of their consumption of human food, fled its parks as a result of flying bombs in 1944. Tree-felling, for example for airfields, reduced the number of sparrows. Some birds did, however, benefit from the war. Bomb craters yielded additional food sources, as did the partial conversion of golf courses to allotments. Avocets returned to the East Anglian marshes, which had been reflooded as part of the nation's defence.

Messenger pigeons had been important in the First World War. Given the improved interwar communications, by the Second

Boxes of carrier pigeons, ready to do their bit for the war effort.

World War these birds were deemed to be redundant. But when water-damaged radios in downed aircraft failed to work, a civilian National Pigeon Service was established. During the war pigeon fanciers provided 200,000 birds – nearly twice the number offered in 1914–18. Many were either assigned to Bomber Command in watertight containers or employed to carry messages from the Resistance. Whenever an aircrew ditched into the sea, the plane's pigeon would be released to aid rescue. The pigeon would return home with details of the plane's last known coordinates and the flight's coded identity.

Over 16,000 pigeons were parachuted individually or by agent into occupied Europe. German countermeasures (hawks and guns) meant, however, that fewer than 2,000 pigeons returned. Homing pigeons also encountered danger in Britain – from falcons that dive-bombed them at 200mph (pigeons fly at 80mph). As a result, the government encouraged the destruction of falcons and their nests.

A message written on rice paper is put into a container and attached to a carrier pigeon by members of 61st Division Signals in Northern Ireland, 1941.

ANIMAL WAR HEROES

Although animals clearly suffered because of the war, it could be argued that they also contributed to the war effort. Such contributions were evident on the Home Front and on active service, and included maintaining morale, relaying information, preventing harm or acting as guinea pigs in the service of military science, which sought to anticipate and counteract possible developments in (German) chemical warfare. Occasionally animals were honoured for their contribution.

Judy was the mascot of HMS Grasshopper. *When the ship was hit by torpedoes in 1942, she and the surviving crew managed to land at Sumatra, where they all became prisoners of war.*

Britain neither suffered nor inflicted biological warfare but prepared itself in case Germany did. Porton Down in Wiltshire was the national chemical warfare centre, but there were other sites. In 1942 on Gruinard Island, off the Scottish coast, experiments were undertaken with munitions charged with anthrax spores. Infected bombs were deliberately exploded close to 80 sheep, which contracted anthrax and died within days.

Operation Vegetarian took place here, too. Cattle were fed anthrax-infected linseed cakes. It was intended that such cakes would be dropped on German pasturelands to be consumed by livestock to subsequently poison the population. The test succeeded and five million anthrax cakes were manufactured but never used. At Porton Down goats were successfully exposed to modified grenade charges whereby seemingly non-lethal wounds inflicted by their explosion would nevertheless still prove fatal.

The Blue Cross Fund first awarded medals to honour warhorses in 1918. In 1940 the Fund was re-established and the award widened to include other animals. Recipients included a French dog, La Cloche, who was awarded for saving her master from the *Meknes*, a French liner torpedoed by Germany. Fluff the dog was also honoured because she had alerted others to her owners who had been buried alive in the rubble of their bombed house. The Great Dane Juliana was awarded the medal twice. In 1941 she extinguished an incendiary bomb in her owner's house by urinating on it, and in 1944 she alerted others to a fire in her owner's shop. She was poisoned anonymously in 1946.

In January 1943 Maria Dickin, founder of PDSA, established the PDSA Dickin Medal. Its purpose was also to honour the work of animals during the war. It became known as the 'animals' VC'. A bronze medallion bearing the words 'For Gallantry' and 'We Also Serve' was awarded to those animals 'displaying conspicuous gallantry or devotion to duty' as part of the armed forces or Civil Defence units. Those selected during the war were horses, dogs, a cat and, above all, pigeons. Most were to be honoured after the war.

Judy was awarded the PDSA Dickin Medal in 1946 for her actions during internment. It is decorated with an embossed laurel leaf border and the text: 'PDSA For Gallantry We Also Serve'.

Air-Raid Precautions dog Rip searches through brick rubble and timber for survivors following an air raid in Poplar, London, in 1941.

AFTERMATH AND REMEMBRANCE

The war ended in 1945. Demobilisation and the return of peace impacted on animals and those connected with them. These ranged from formal ceremonies to the return of dog shows and press advertisements for branded pet food such as Chappie.

In 1945 the ceremony marking the end of the Civil Defence's wartime role included two rescue dogs and their trainers. The training and use of dogs for military purposes would continue, however. In August 1946 mine detector dogs working in Germany were transferred to what was then Palestine to locate terrorist arms. Although initially only strays, often other dogs in Germany, many requisitioned, were humanely destroyed.

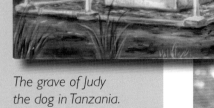

The grave of Judy the dog in Tanzania.

Rip the dog receives his PDSA Dickin Medal (awarded 1945).

Military dog handlers were instructed not to make pets of their charges. But mutual attachment often developed and they, as with other overseas service personnel who had befriended animals, often wanted the animal to return to Britain with them. Eventually the War Office's Veterinary Department established a reception centre for soldiers' pet dogs and met most of the quarantine costs. The RSPCA supplied equipment for any dogs requiring medical attention.

Some 1,500 war dogs were returned to Britain and many were restored to their owners. Others were less fortunate. Of the 17 dogs awarded the RSPCA For Valour medal, only three came back from military service overseas.

A memorial to Mary the racing pigeon, who was awarded the PDSA Dickin Medal for outstanding service during the war.

Most recipients of the PDSA Dickin Medal received their award between 1943 and 1949. Olga was one of three London police horses to be so honoured. Despite initially bolting because of a bomb explosion in July 1944, she had returned to the site and resumed her traffic-control duties to assist the rescue services. Of the 18 dogs honoured, one was Brian – a paradog, dropped into France during the D-Day landings. One of the most celebrated of the 32 PDSA Dickin Medal pigeons was GI Joe. Flying at 60mph, his message prevented 100 Allied soldiers from being bombed by their own planes.

There are memorials to animals in the Second World War. One notable example is the Animals in War memorial in Park Lane, London, which was unveiled in 2004. To date, there is no memorial to those animals that perished in September 1939. The RAVC holds an Animals in War Memorial Service in Westminster Abbey close to Remembrance Sunday. It also has memorials near the Animal Defence Centre in Leicestershire and the National Memorial Arboretum, Staffordshire.

But also located in the Arboretum is a Civil Defence memorial. It, too, honours the 'animal friends who served with such loyalty and bravery' – a fitting tribute and conclusion.

PLACES TO VISIT

Imperial War Museum
IWM London, Lambeth Road, London, SE1 6HZ
www.IWM.org.uk

National Army Museum
Royal Hospital Road, Chelsea, London, SW3 4HT
www.nam.ac.uk/research/famous-units/
royal-army-veterinary-corps

**The Museum of Military Medicine
(for the Royal Army Veterinary Corps)**
Keogh Barracks, Aldershot, GU12 5RQ
www.museumofmilitarymedicine.org.uk

Royal Air Force Museum
Grahame Park Way, London, NW9 5LL
www.rafmuseum.org.uk

Ilford/PDSA Animal Cemetery
Woodford Bridge Road, Redbridge, Ilford, Essex, IG4 5PS
www.pdsa.org.uk

National Memorial Arboretum
Croxall Road, Alrewas, Staffordshire, DE13 7AR
www.thenma.org.uk

Animals in War Memorial
Brook Gate, Park Lane, London, W1
www.animalsinwar.org.uk

The Royal Army Veterinary Corps memorial at the National Memorial Arboretum in Staffordshire.